Congressional Research Service

Access to Broadband Networks: The Net Neutrality Debate

Angele A. Gilroy
Specialist in Telecommunications Policy

September 17, 2012

Congressional Research Service
7-5700
www.crs.gov
R40616

CRS Report for Congress ──────────
Prepared for Members and Committees of Congress

Summary

As congressional policymakers continue to debate telecommunications reform, a major point of contention is the question of whether action is needed to ensure unfettered access to the Internet. The move to place restrictions on the owners of the networks that compose and provide access to the Internet, to ensure equal access and non-discriminatory treatment, is referred to as "net neutrality." While there is no single accepted definition of "net neutrality," most agree that any such definition should include the general principles that owners of the networks that compose and provide access to the Internet should not control how consumers lawfully use that network, and they should not be able to discriminate against content provider access to that network.

A major focus in the debate is concern over whether it is necessary for policymakers to take steps to ensure access to the Internet for content, services, and applications providers, as well as consumers, and if so, what these steps should be. Some policymakers contend that more specific regulatory guidelines may be necessary to protect the marketplace from potential abuses which could threaten the net neutrality concept. Others contend that existing laws and policies are sufficient to deal with potential anti-competitive behavior and that additional regulations would have negative effects on the expansion and future development of the Internet. The December 21, 2010, adoption, and November 20, 2011, implementation, by the Federal Communications Commission (FCC) of its Open Internet Order has focused attention on the issue. Although most concede that networks have always needed and will continue to need some management, the use of prioritization tools, such as deep packet inspection, as well as the initiation of metered/usage-based billing practices have further fueled the debate.

A consensus on the net neutrality issue has remained elusive and support for the FCC's Open Internet Order has been mixed. While some Members of Congress support the action, and in some cases would have supported an even stronger approach, others feel that the FCC has overstepped its authority and that the regulation of the Internet is not only unnecessary, but harmful. Internet regulation and the FCC's authority to implement such regulations has been a topic of legislation (H.R. 96, H.R. 166, S. 74, H.R. 2434, H.R. 1, H.R. 3630, H.J.Res. 37, and S.J.Res. 6) and hearings in the 112th Congress. The House, on April 8, 2011, passed (240-179) H.J.Res. 37, to state disapproval of and remove the force and effect of the FCC's Open Internet Order. However, an identical resolution of disapproval (S.J.Res. 6) failed to pass the Senate on November 10, 2011, by a 52-46 vote. Attempts to prohibit implementation through the appropriations process, by the withholding of FCC funds for such purposes, have also been unsuccessful. It is anticipated that the issue of Internet access will be of continued interest to policymakers.

The net neutrality issue has also been narrowly addressed within the context of the American Recovery and Reinvestment Act of 2009 (ARRA, P.L. 111-5). Provisions required the National Telecommunications and Information Administration (NTIA), in consultation with the FCC, to establish "nondiscrimination and network interconnection obligations" as a requirement for grant participants in the Broadband Technology Opportunities Program (BTOP). These obligations were released, July 1, 2009, in conjunction with the issuance of a notice of funds availability soliciting applications. Recipients of these awards have been selected and continued congressional oversight is expected.

The ARRA also required the FCC to submit a report, containing a national broadband plan, to both the House and Senate Commerce Committees; it was released on March 16, 2010.

Contents

Contacts

Introduction

As congressional policymakers continue to debate telecommunications reform, a major point of contention is the question of whether action is needed to ensure unfettered access to the Internet. The move to place restrictions on the owners of the networks that compose and provide access to the Internet, to ensure equal access and non-discriminatory treatment, is referred to as "net neutrality." There is no single accepted definition of "net neutrality." However, most agree that any such definition should include the general principles that owners of the networks that compose and provide access to the Internet should not control how consumers lawfully use that network, and they should not be able to discriminate against content provider access to that network.

What, if any, action should be taken to ensure "net neutrality" has become a major focal point in the debate over broadband regulation. As the marketplace for broadband continues to evolve, some contend that no new regulations are needed, and if enacted will slow deployment of and access to the Internet, as well as limit innovation. Others, however, contend that the consolidation and diversification of broadband providers into content providers has the potential to lead to discriminatory behaviors which conflict with net neutrality principles. The two potential behaviors most often cited are the network providers' ability to control access to and the pricing of broadband facilities, and the incentive to favor network-owned content, thereby placing unaffiliated content providers at a competitive disadvantage.

Federal Communications Commission Activity

The Information Services Designation and Title I

In 2005 two major actions dramatically changed the regulatory landscape as it applied to broadband services, further fueling the net neutrality debate. In both cases these actions led to the classification of broadband Internet access services as Title I information services, thereby subjecting them to a less rigorous regulatory framework than those services classified as telecommunications services. In the first action, the U.S. Supreme Court, in a June 2005 decision (*National Cable & Telecommunications Association v. Brand X Internet Services*), upheld the Federal Communications Commission's (FCC's) 2002 ruling that the provision of cable modem service (i.e., cable television broadband Internet) is an interstate information service and is therefore subject to the less stringent regulatory regime under Title I of the Communications Act of 1934.[1] In a second action, the FCC, in an August 5, 2005, decision, extended the same regulatory relief to telephone company Internet access services (i.e., wireline broadband Internet access, or DSL), thereby also defining such services as information services subject to Title I regulation.[2] As a result neither telephone companies nor cable companies, when providing broadband services, are required to adhere to the more stringent regulatory regime for

---

[1] 47 U.S.C. 151 et seq. For a full discussion of the Brand X decision see CRS Report RL32985, *Defining Cable Broadband Internet Access Service: Background and Analysis of the Supreme Court's Brand X Decision*, by Angie A. Welborn and Charles B. Goldfarb.

[2] See http://hraunfoss.fcc.gov/edocs_public/attachmatch/DOC-260433A2.pdf for a copy of former FCC Chairman Martin's statement. For a summary of the final rule see Appropriate Framework for Broadband Access to the Internet Over Wireline Facilities. *Federal Register*, Vol. 70, No. 199, October 17, 2005, p. 60222.

telecommunications services found under Title II (common carrier) of the 1934 act.[3] However, classification as an information service does not free the service from regulation. The FCC continues to have regulatory authority over information services under its Title I, ancillary jurisdiction.[4] Similarly classification under Title II does not mean that an entity will be subject to the full range of regulatory requirements as the FCC is given the authority, under Section 10 of the Communications Act of 1934, to forbear from regulation.

The 2005 Internet Policy Statement

Simultaneous to the issuing of its August 2005 information services classification order, the FCC also adopted a policy statement (Internet Policy Statement) outlining four principles to "encourage broadband deployment and preserve and promote the open and interconnected nature of [the] public Internet." The four principles are (1) consumers are entitled to access the lawful Internet content of their choice; (2) consumers are entitled to run applications and services of their choice (subject to the needs of law enforcement); (3) consumers are entitled to connect their choice of legal devices that do not harm the network; and (4) consumers are entitled to competition among network providers, application and service providers, and content providers. Then-FCC Chairman Martin did not call for their codification. However, he stated that they would be incorporated into the policymaking activities of the commission.[5] For example, one of the agreed upon conditions for the October 2005 approval of both the Verizon/MCI and the SBC/AT&T mergers was an agreement made by the involved parties to commit, for two years, "to conduct business in a way that comports with the commission's (2005) Internet policy statement."[6] In a further action AT&T included in its concessions to gain FCC approval of its merger to BellSouth to adhering, for two years, to significant net neutrality requirements. Under terms of the merger agreement, which was approved on December 29, 2006, AT&T agreed to not only uphold, for 30 months, the FCC's Internet policy statement principles, but also committed, for two years (expired December 2008), to stringent requirements to "maintain a neutral network and neutral routing in its wireline broadband Internet access service."[7]

FCC Chairman Genachowski announced, in a September 21, 2009, speech,[8] a proposal to consider the expansion and codification of the 2005 Internet Policy Statement and suggested that this be accomplished through a notice of proposed rulemaking (NPR) process. Shortly thereafter an NPR on preserving the open Internet and broadband industry practices was adopted by the FCC in its October 22, 2009, meeting. (See "The FCC Open Internet Order," below.)

---

[3] For example, Title II regulations impose rigorous anti-discrimination, interconnection and access requirements. For a further discussion of Title I versus Title II regulatory authority see CRS Report RL32985, *Defining Cable Broadband Internet Access Service: Background and Analysis of the Supreme Court's Brand X Decision.*

[4] Title I of the 1934 Communications Act gives the FCC such authority if assertion of jurisdiction is "reasonably ancillary to the effective performance of [its] various responsibilities." The FCC in its order cites consumer protection, network reliability, or national security obligations as examples of cases where such authority would apply (see paragraph 36 of the final rule summarized in the *Federal Register* cite in footnote 2, above).

[5] See http://www.fcc.gov/headlines2005.html. August 5, 2005. *FCC Adopts Policy Statement on Broadband Internet Access.*

[6] See http://hraunfoss.FCC.gov/edocs_public/attachmatch/DOC-261936A1.pdf. It should be noted that applicants offered certain voluntary commitments, of which this was one.

[7] See http://hraunfoss.fcc.gov/edocs_public/attachmatch/DOC-269275A1.pdf.

[8] *"Preserving a Free and Open Internet: A Platform for Innovation, Opportunity, and Prosperity,"* prepared remarks of FCC Chairman Julius Genachowski, at the Brookings Institution, September 21, 2009. Available at http://hraunfoss.fcc.gov/edocs_public/attachmatch/DOC-293568A1.pdf.

The FCC August 2008 Comcast Decision

In perhaps one of its most significant actions relating to its Internet Policy Statement to date, the FCC, on August 1, 2008, ruled that Comcast Corp., a provider of Internet access over cable lines, violated the FCC's policy statement when it selectively blocked peer-to-peer connections in an attempt to manage its traffic.[9] This practice, the FCC concluded, "unduly interfered with Internet users' rights to access the lawful Internet content and to use the applications of their choice." Although no monetary penalties were imposed, Comcast was required to stop these practices by the end of 2008. Comcast complied with the order, and developed a new system to manage network congestion. Comcast no longer manages congestion by focusing on specific applications (such as peer-to-peer), nor by focusing on online activities, or protocols, but identifies individual users within congested neighborhoods that are using large amounts of bandwidth in real time and slows them down, by placing them in a lower priority category, for short periods.[10] This new system complies with the FCC Internet principles in that it is application agnostic; that is, it does not discriminate against or favor one application over another but manages congestion based on the amount of a user's real-time bandwidth usage. As a result of a April 6, 2010, court ruling the FCC's order was vacated. Comcast, however, has stated that it will continue to comply with the Internet principles issued in the FCC's August 2005 Internet policy statement.[11] (See "Comcast v. FCC," below.)

Comcast v. FCC

Despite compliance, however, Comcast filed an appeal[12] in the U.S. Court of Appeals for the District of Columbia, claiming that the FCC did not have the authority to enforce its Internet policy statement, therefore making the order invalid. The FCC argued that while it did not have express statutory authority over such practices, it derived such authority based on its ancillary authority contained in Title I of the 1934 Communications Act.[13] The court, in an April 6, 2010, decision, ruled (3-0) that the FCC did not have the authority to regulate an Internet service provider's (in this case Comcast's) network management practices and vacated the FCC's order.[14] The court ruled that the exercise of ancillary authority must be linked to statutory authority and that the FCC did not in its arguments prove that connection; it cannot exercise ancillary authority based on policy alone. More specifically, the Court ruled that the FCC "failed to tie its assertion of ancillary authority over Comcast's Internet service to any ["statutorily mandated responsibility"]."[15] Based on that conclusion the court granted the petition for review and vacated the order.

---

[9] See http://hraunfoss.fcc.gov/edocs_public/attachmatch/FCC-08-183A1.pdf.

[10] Comcast, *Frequently Asked Questions and Network Management.* Available at http://help.comcast.net/content/faq/Frequently-Asked-Questions-about-Network-Management.

[11] *Comcast Statement on U.S. Court of Appeals Decision on Comcast v. FCC.* Available at http://www.comcast.com/About/PressRelease/PressReleaseDetail.ashx?PRID=984.

[12] Comcast Corporation v. FCC, No. 08-129 (D.C. Cir. September 4, 2008).

[13] For a legal discussion of the FCC's regulatory authority in light of the Comcast decision see CRS Report R40234, *The FCC's Authority to Regulate Net Neutrality After Comcast v. FCC,* by Kathleen Ann Ruane.

[14] Comcast Corporation v. FCC decided April 6, 2010. Available at http://pacer.cadc.uscourts.gov/common/opinions/201004/08-1291-1238302.pdf.

[15] Comcast v. FCC decision, issued April 6, 2010, part V, p. 36.

The impact of this decision on the FCC's ability to regulate broadband services and implement its broadband policy goals remains unclear. Regardless of the path that is taken FCC Chairman Genachowski has stated that the court decision "does not change our broadband policy goals, or the ultimate authority of the FCC to act to achieve those goals." He further stated that "[T]he court did not question the FCC's goals; it merely invalidated one, technical, legal mechanism for broadband policy chosen by prior Commissions."[16] Consistent with this statement, the FCC in a December 21, 2010, action adopted the Open Internet Order to establish rules to maintain network neutrality (see "The FCC Open Internet Order").

The FCC Open Internet Order

The FCC adopted, on December 21, 2010, an Open Internet Order establishing rules to govern the network management practices of broadband Internet access providers.[17] The order, which was passed by a 3-2 vote,[18] intends to maintain network neutrality by establishing three rules covering transparency,[19] no blocking, and no unreasonable discrimination. More specifically:

- fixed and mobile broadband Internet service providers are required to publically disclose accurate information regarding network management practices, performance, and commercial terms to consumers and as well as content, application, service, and device providers;

- fixed and mobile broadband Internet service providers are both subject, to varying degrees, to no blocking requirements. Fixed providers are prohibited from blocking lawful content, applications, services, or non-harmful devices, subject to reasonable network management. Mobile providers are prohibited from blocking consumers from accessing lawful websites, subject to reasonable network management, nor can they block applications that compete with the provider's voice or video telephony services, subject to reasonable network management;

- fixed broadband Internet service providers are subject to a "no unreasonable discrimination rule" that states that they shall not unreasonably discriminate in transmitting lawful network traffic over a consumer's broadband Internet access service. Reasonable network management shall not constitute unreasonable discrimination.[20]

---

[16] FCC Announces Broadband Action Agenda, released April 8, 2010. Available at http://hraunfoss.fcc.gov/edocs_public/attachmatch/DOC-297402A1.pdf.

[17] *In the Matter of Preserving the Open Internet, Broadband Industry Practices.* GN Docket No. 09-191; WC Docket No. 07-52, released December 23, 2010. Available at http://www.fcc.gov/Daily_Releases/Daily_Business/2010/db1223/FCC-10-201A1.pdf.

[18] The vote fell along party lines with Chairman Genachowski approving, Commissioner Clyburn approving in part and concurring in part, former Commissioner Copps concurring, and Commissioner McDowell and former Commissioner Baker dissenting.

[19] The FCC, on June 30, 2011, released a public notice offering initial guidance regarding compliance with the transparency rule. *FCC Enforcement Bureau and Office Of General Counsel Issue Advisory Guidance For Compliance With Open Internet Transparency Rule.* Available at http://hraunfoss.fcc.gov/edocs_public/attachmatch/DA-11-1148A1.pdf.

[20] A network management practice is considered reasonable if "it is appropriate and tailored to achieving a legitimate network management purpose, taking in to account the particular network architecture and technology of the broadband Internet access service." Cited examples include ensuring network security and integrity; providing parental controls; (continued...)

Additional provisions in the order include those which provide for ongoing monitoring of the mobile broadband sector and create an Open Internet Advisory Committee[21] to track and evaluate the effects of the rules and provide recommendations to the FCC regarding open Internet policies and practices; while not banning paid prioritization, state it is unlikely to satisfy the "no unreasonable discrimination" rule; raise concerns about specialized services and while not "adopting policies specific to such services at this time," will closely monitor such services; call for review, and possible adjustment, of all rules in the order no later than two years from their effective date; and detail a formal and informal complaint process. The order, however, does not prohibit tiered or usage-based pricing (see "Metered/Usage-Based Billing," below). According to the order, the framework "... does not prevent broadband providers from asking subscribers who use the network less to pay less, and subscribers who use the network more to pay more" since prohibiting such practices "... would force lighter end users of the network to subsidize heavier end users" and "... would also foreclose practices that may appropriately align incentives to encourage efficient use of networks."[22]

The authority to adopt the order abandons the "third way approach" previously endorsed by Chairman Genachowski and other Democratic commissioners,[23] and treats broadband Internet access service as an information service under Title I. The order relies on a number of provisions contain in the 1934 Communications Act, as amended, to support FCC authority. According to the order the authority to implement these rules lies in Section 706 of the 1996 Telecommunications Act, which directs the FCC to "encourage the deployment on a reasonable and timely basis" of "advanced telecommunications capability" to all Americans and to take action if it finds that such capability is not being deployed in a reasonable and timely fashion;[24] Title II of the Communications Act and its role in protecting competition and consumers of telecommunications services; Title III, which gives the FCC the authority to license spectrum, subject to terms that serve the public interest, used to provide fixed and mobile wireless services; and Title VI, which gives the FCC the duty to protect competition in video services.

The order went into effect November 20, 2011, which was 60 days after its publication in the *Federal Register*.[25] Since the Order's publication multiple appeals have been filed and subsequently consolidated for review in the U.S. Court of Appeals, D.C. Circuit.[26] Verizon

---

(...continued)

or reducing or mitigating the effects of congestion on the network.

[21] The FCC announced the creation of an Open Internet Advisory Committee April 21, 2011, *Federal Register*, Vol. 76, No. 77, April 21, 2011, p. 22395. The Committee, which includes members from a broad range of industry, academic, and community representatives, held its first meeting in July 2012.

[22] *In the Matter of Preserving the Open Internet, Broadband Industry Practices,* paragraph 72.

[23] This approach consists of pursuing a bifurcated, or separate, regulatory approach by applying the specific provisions of Title II to the transmission component of broadband access service and subjecting the information component to, at most, whatever ancillary jurisdiction may exist under Title I. See *The Third Way: A Narrowly Tailored Broadband Framework*, FCC Chairman Julius Genachowski, May 6, 2010. Available at http://hraunfoss.fcc.gov/edocs_public/ attachmatch/DOC-297944A1.pdf. Also see *A Third-Way Legal Framework for Addressing the Comcast Dilemma*, Austin Schlick, FCC General Counsel, May 6, 2010. Available at http://hraunfoss.fcc.gov/edocs_public/attachmatch/ DOC-297945A1.pdf.

[24] The FCC made such a finding, that is that "broadband is not being deployed to all Americans in a reasonable and timely fashion" in its *Sixth Broadband Deployment Report*, adopted on July 16, 2010. Available at http://www.fcc.gov/ Daily_Releases/Daily_Business/2010/db0720/FCC-10-129A1.pdf.

[25] Preserving the Open Internet; Final Rule. *Federal Register*, Vol.76, No. 185, September 23, 2011, pp. 59192-59235.

[26] Order Granting Mot. Cons., DC/1:11-ca-01356, (J.P.M.L., October 6, 2011).

Communications and MetroPCS Communications are once again seeking review[27] claiming, among issues, that it is a violation of free speech and that the FCC has exceeded its authority in establishing the rules.[28] The briefing schedule commenced on July 2, 2012, and concludes on November 21, 2012. A date for oral arguments is yet to be set.

The American Recovery and Reinvestment Act of 2009

The FCC has also been called upon to address net neutrality principles within the context of the implementation of the American Recovery and Reinvestment Act of 2009 (ARRA, P.L. 111-5). Provisions require the National Telecommunications and Information Administration (NTIA), in consultation with the FCC, to establish "nondiscrimination and network interconnection obligations" as a requirement for grant participants in the Broadband Technology Opportunities Program (BTOP). These obligations were issued July 1, 2009, in conjunction with the release of the notice of funds availability (NOFA) soliciting applications for the program.[29] The NOFA requires that recipients of both ARRA programs (the Rural Utilities Service Broadband Initiative Program (BIP) as well as the mandated BTOP program) adhere to these requirements,[30] and expands requirements beyond those contained in the FCC's 2005 Internet Policy Statement. More specifically award recipients are required to adhere to the FCC's 2005 Internet Policy Statement; not favor any lawful Internet applications and content over others; display network management policies on their web pages and provide notice to customers of changes to these policies; connect to the public Internet directly or indirectly (that is, the project can not be an entirely private closed network); and "offer interconnection, where technically feasible without exceeding current or reasonably anticipated capacity limitations, on reasonable rates and terms to be negotiated with requesting parties." Recipients of these awards have been selected, projects are being deployed, and congressional oversight is ongoing.

The FCC's National Broadband Plan

The ARRA also required the FCC to submit a report, containing a national broadband plan, to both the House and Senate Commerce Committees. The report, *Connecting America: The National Broadband Plan* (NBP), was released on March 16, 2010.[31] The NBP did not contain specific recommendations regarding the debate over access to broadband networks, but Chapter 4 did discuss the value of an open Internet. The NBP referred to the FCC's then-ongoing notice of

---

[27] Earlier appeals by both companies were filed but dismissed by the court. See *Verizon v. FCC* D.C. Cir. 11-1014, 1/20/2011; and *MetroPCS Communications et. al. v. FCC* D.C. Cir.11-1016, 1/24/2011. The U.S. Court of Appeals, on April 4, 2011, rejected both filings as premature, stating that the Order is a rulemaking and therefore must first be published in the *Federal Register* before it can be subject to judicial review *Verizon v. FCC*, Order Granting Mot. Dismiss, Case No.11-1014 (D.C. Cir. April 4, 2011).

[28] *Verizon v. FCC,* D.C. Cir. 11-1355, 10/18/2011 and *MetroPCS Communications, Inc. v. FCC*, D.C. Cir. 11-1403, 10/21/2011.

[29] For additional details on the NOFA see Department of Agriculture, Rural Utilities Service, and Department of Commerce, National Telecommunications and Information Administration, "Broadband Initiatives Program; Broadband Technology Opportunities Program; Notice," 74 *Federal Register* 33104 -33134, July 9, 2009.

[30] As of October 1, 2010, all BTOP and BIP award announcements were complete. For a review of ARRA programs and a listing of awards granted see CRS Report R40436, *Broadband Infrastructure Programs in the American Recovery and Reinvestment Act*, by Lennard G. Kruger.

[31] *Connecting America: The National Broadband Plan.* Available at http://hraunfoss.fcc.gov/edocs_public/attachmatch/DOC-296935A1.pdf.

---

proposed rulemaking on Preserving the Open Internet (see "The FCC Open Internet Order," above) and stated that "broadband's ability to derive the many benefits discussed in this plan depend[s] on its continued openness."[32]

One other issue relevant to the open access/net neutrality debate focuses on the regulatory classification of broadband services. Chapter 17 of the NBP provides a discussion of the legal framework for the plan's implementation. While the discussion does not reach any conclusions regarding the appropriate framework, it does outline the debate over whether broadband services should retain its Title I classification as an information service, or should be classified as a telecommunications service under Title II.[33] (See "The Information Services Designation and Title I," above.) While the NBP does not reach a conclusion regarding classification, some feel it does open up the door for discussion[34] by concluding that "the FCC will consider these and related questions as it moves forward to implement the plan."[35] Since the NBP's release, however, the FCC, in its Open Internet Order, adopted in December 2010, concluded that such services would remain under Title I classification. (See "The FCC Open Internet Order," above.)

Additional Activity

In a June 17, 2010, action the FCC adopted a notice of inquiry (NOI), which is still pending, to examine the framework for broadband Internet service. The NOI (General Docket No.10-127) seeks comment on issues such as broadband Internet classification, and the proper role of the states with respect to broadband Internet service.[36] Separately, in an April 2007 action, the FCC released a notice of inquiry (WC Docket No. 07-52), on broadband industry practices seeking comment on a wide range of issues including whether the August 2005 Internet policy statement should be amended to incorporate a new principle of nondiscrimination and if so, what form it should take.[37] On January 14, 2008, the FCC issued three public notices seeking comment on issues related to network management (including the now-completed Comcast ruling, discussed above) and held two (February 25 and April 17, 2008) public hearings specific to broadband network management practices.

Certain restrictions on the operation and management of Comcast's Internet facilities were agreed to as a condition of the January 18, 2011, approval by the Department of Justice (DOJ) and the

---

[32] *Connecting America: The National Broadband Plan*, Chapter 4, Broadband Competition and Innovation Policy, Section 4.4, Competition for Value Across the Ecosystem.

[33] It should be noted that the FCC is given the authority, under §10 of the 1934 Communications Act, to forbear from regulation, therefore, if such a reclassification should occur, all requirements of a Title II classification would not necessarily be imposed.

[34] See, for example, Statement of FCC Commissioner Robert McDowell, before the Committee on Energy and Commerce, Subcommittee on Communications, Technology, and the Internet, hearing on Oversight of the Federal Communications Commission: The National Broadband Plan, March 25, 2010. available at http://hraunfoss.fcc.gov/edocs_public/attachmatch/DOC-297139A1.pdf.

[35] *Connecting America: The National Broadband Plan*, Chapter 17, Implementation and Benchmarks, Section 17.3, The Legal Framework for the FCC's Implementation of the Plan. The FCC released a "2010 Broadband Action Agenda" on April 8, 2010, containing a timeframe for FCC proceedings to help implement the plan. A summary table of proposed 2010 agenda items is available at http://www.broadband.gov/plan/chart-of-key-broadband-action-agenda-items.pdf.

[36] *In the Matter of Framework for Broadband Internet Service*, General Docket No. 10-127. Available at http://hraunfoss.fcc.gov/edocs_public/attachmatch/FCC-10-114A1.pdf.

[37] *Broadband Industry Practices*, WC Docket No. 07-52, Notice of Inquiry, 22 FCC Record 7894 (2007).

FCC, of the merger between Comcast Corp. and NBC Universal Inc.[38] For example, Section V.G of the DOJ Final Judgment enumerates restrictions that Comcast has agreed to abide by regarding its Internet facilities. Open access requirements, consistent with the FCC's Open Internet Order, were agreed to as part of the settlement. More specifically, Comcast is prohibited from unreasonably discriminating in the transmission of an OVD's (online video distributors) lawful network traffic to a Comcast broadband customer.[39] Additional restrictions include those which: prohibit Comcast from excluding its own services from any caps, tiers, metering, or other usage based plans and requires that OVD traffic be counted in the same way as Comcast's traffic to ensure that billing plans are not used to disadvantage an OVD; prohibits Comcast from offering specialized services that are comprised substantially or entirely of its own or its affiliates services; and if offering specialized services must offer similar specialized services on a nondiscriminatory basis. The DOJ Final judgment and the FCC Order stay in force for seven years (January 2018).

Industry Initiatives

Industry stakeholders have also taken the initiative to address broadband policy issues by establishing voluntary discussion groups and frameworks to further the debate. For example, a voluntary working group comprised of Internet service providers, content, applications, hardware makers, and community representatives announced the establishment of a technical advisory group of engineers to address technical issues surrounding the net neutrality debate. The major mission of this working group, called the Broadband Internet Technical Advisory Group (BITAG), is to develop consensus on voluntary industry guidelines to address industry technical standards relating to broadband network management practices or other related issues that can affect users' Internet experience. The BITAG mission could also include "(1) educating policymakers on technical issues; (2) attempting to address specific technical matters in an effort to minimize related policy disputes; and (3) serving as a sounding board for new ideas and network management practices."[40] BITAG, an independent non-profit organization, announced on December 16, 2010, the appointment of an interim board of directors and the commencement of a Technical Working Group to address substantive issues.[41]

Two major stakeholders, Verizon and Google, announced on August 9, 2010, a proposal containing a suggested "open Internet framework for the consideration of policymakers and the public."[42] Some of the key elements of the proposal, which was offered in the form of a suggested "legislative framework," include

---

[38] *United States, et. al. v. Comcast Corp., et. al.*; Proposed Final Judgment and Competitive Impact Statement; Notice. Federal Register, Vol. 76, No. 20, January 31, 2011, pp.5440-5464. In the Matter of Applications of Comcast Corporation, General Electric Company and NBC Universal, Inc. For Consent to Assign Licenses and Transfer Control of Licenses, MB Docket No. 10-56. available at http://www.fcc.gov/Fcc-11-4.pdf.

[39] "Reasonable network management shall not constitute unreasonable discrimination."

[40] *Initial Plans for Broadband Internet Technical Advisory Group Announced.* PRNewswire, June 9, 2010. Available at http://www.prnewswire.com/news-releases/initial-plans-for-broadband-internet-technical-advisory-group-announced-95950.

[41] BITAG's Interim Board of Directors Announced; First Board Meeting Scheduled for Next Week. Available at http://log.bitag.org/2010/12/bitags-interim-board-of-directors.html.

[42] *Verizon-Google Legislative Framework Proposal.* Available at http://www.scribd.com/doc/35599242/verizon-google-legislative-framework-proposal.

- broadband Internet access service providers would be prohibited from preventing their users from sending and receiving lawful content of their choice, running lawful applications and using lawful services of their choice, and connecting their choice of legal devices;

- broadband Internet access providers would be prohibited from engaging in undue discrimination against any lawful Internet content, application, or service that causes meaningful harm to competition or users;

- providers of broadband Internet access service would be subject to disclosure and transparency requirements so that consumers and others could make informed choices;

- broadband Internet access service providers are permitted to engage in reasonable network management;

- a provider who is complying with these principles could offer any other additional or differentiated services that could include traffic prioritization;

- the FCC would enforce consumer protection and nondiscrimination requirements on a case-by-case basis and could impose a forfeiture of up to $2 million for knowing violations;

- the FCC would have exclusive authority over broadband Internet access service but would have no authority over Internet software applications, content, or services;

- broadband Internet access service and traffic or services using Internet protocol would be considered exclusively interstate in nature;

- broadband Internet access would be eligible for Federal universal service support to spur deployment in unserved areas and adoption by low-income populations; and

- wireless networks would only be subject to the transparency principle at this time.

Industry stakeholders have also participated in talks conducted by the FCC and designated congressional committees of jurisdiction. The FCC talks, which consisted of a series of meetings with various industry stakeholders to discuss communications issues with a particular focus on the broadband reclassification issue, concluded in the summer of 2010, without reaching a consensus. Congressional sessions held in the 111th Congress, by the Senate Commerce and the House Energy and Commerce Committees and their Communications Subcommittees, covered the topics of broadband regulation/consumer protection and FCC authority; spectrum policy; and broadband deployment and adoption; no further action was taken.

Network Management

As consumers expand their use of the Internet and new multimedia and voice services become more commonplace, control over network quality and pricing is an issue. The ability of data bits to travel the network in a nondiscriminatory manner (subject to reasonable management practices), as well as the pricing structure established by broadband service providers for consumer access to that data, have become significant issues in the debate.

Prioritization

In the past, Internet traffic has been delivered on a "best efforts" basis. The quality of service needed for the delivery of the most popular uses, such as e-mail or surfing the web, is not as dependent on guaranteed quality. However, as Internet use expands to include video, online gaming, and voice service, the need for uninterrupted streams of data becomes important. As the demand for such services continues to expand, network broadband operators are moving to prioritize network traffic to ensure the quality of these services. Prioritization may benefit consumers by ensuring faster delivery and quality of service and may be necessary to ensure the proper functioning of expanded service options. However, the move on the part of network operators to establish prioritized networks, although embraced by some, has led to a number of policy concerns.

There is concern that the ability of network providers to prioritize traffic may give them too much power over the operation of, and access to, the Internet. If a multi-tiered Internet develops where content providers pay for different service levels, the potential to limit competition exists if smaller, less financially secure content providers are unable to afford to pay for a higher level of access. Also, if network providers have control over who is given priority access, the ability to discriminate among who gets such access is also present. If such a scenario were to develop, the potential benefits to consumers of a prioritized network would be lessened by a decrease in consumer choice and/or increased costs, if the fees charged for premium access are passed on to the consumer. The potential for these abuses, however, is significantly decreased in a marketplace where multiple, competing broadband providers exist. If a network broadband provider blocks access to content or charges unreasonable fees, in a competitive market, content providers and consumers could obtain their access from other network providers. As consumers and content providers migrate to these competitors, market share and profits of the offending network provider will decrease, leading to corrective action or failure. However, this scenario assumes that every market will have a number of equally competitive broadband options from which to choose, and all competitors will have equal access to, if not identical, at least comparable content.

Deep Packet Inspection

The use of one management tool, deep packet inspection (DPI), illustrates the complexity of the net neutrality debate. DPI refers to a network management technique that enables network operators to inspect, in real time, both the header and the data field of the packets.[43] As a result DPI can allow network operators to not only identify the origin and destination points of the data packet, but also enables the network operator to determine the application used and content of that packet. The information that DPI provides enables the network operator to differentiate, or discriminate, among the packets travelling over its network. The ability to discriminate among packets enables the network operator to treat packets differently. This ability itself is not necessarily viewed in a negative light. Network managers use DPI to assist them in performing various functions that are necessary for network management and that contribute to a positive user experience. For example, DPI technology is used in filters and firewalls to detect and prevent spam, viruses, worms, and malware. DPI is also used to gain information to help plan network

---

[43] The header contains the processing information which includes the source and destination addresses, and the data field includes the message content and the identity of the source application.

capacity and diagnostics, as well as to respond to law enforcement requests.[44] However, the ability to discriminate based on the information gained via DPI also has the potential to be misused.[45] It is the potential negative impact that DPI use can have on consumers and suppliers that raises concern for policymakers. For example, the information gained could be used to discriminate against a competing service causing harm to both the competitor and consumer choice. This could be accomplished by routing a network operator's own, or other preferred content, along a faster priority path, or selectively slowing down competitor's traffic. DPI also has the potential to extract personal information about the data that it inspects, generating concerns about consumer privacy.[46]

Therefore it is not the management tool itself that is under scrutiny, but how it is applied. The DPI technology, in itself, is not what is of concern. It is the behavior that potentially may occur as a result of the information that DPI provides. How to develop a policy that permits some types of discrimination (i.e., "good" discrimination) that may be beneficial to network operation and improve the user experience, while protecting against what would be considered "harmful" or anticompetitive discrimination becomes the crux of the policy debate.

Metered/Usage-Based Billing

The move by some network broadband operators towards the use of metered or usage-based billing has caused considerable controversy. Under such a plan, users subscribe to a set monthly bandwidth cap, for an established fee, and are charged additional fees or could be denied service, if that usage level is exceeded. The use of such billing practices, on both a trial and permanent basis, is becoming more commonplace. Comcast announced the adoption of usage caps for all of its residential customers effective October 1, 2008.[47] Comcast amended its Acceptable Use Policy to establish a specific monthly data usage threshold of 250 GB/month per account for all Xfinity Internet residential customers. Usage above that cap would be considered "excessive" and Comcast will notify and ask the subscriber to moderate their usage.[48] However, in May 2012

---

[44] For a further discussion of the positive uses, by network operators, of DPI technologies see testimony of Kyle McSlarrow, President and CEO National Cable and Telecommunications Association, hearings on "Communications Networks and Consumer Privacy. Recent Developments," House Committee on Energy and Commerce, Subcommittee on Communications, Technology, and the Internet, April 23, 2009. Available at http://energycommercehouse.gov/ Press_111/20090423/testimony_mcslarrow.pdf.

[45] For a further discussion of the potential abuses associated with DPI technology see testimony of Ben Scott, Policy Director, Free Press, hearings on "Communications Networks and Consumer Privacy: Recent Developments," House Committee on Energy and Commerce, Subcommittee on Communications, Technology, and the Internet, April 23, 2009. Available at http://energycommercehouse.gov/Press_111/20090423/testimony_scott.pdf.

[46] For example, concern that information can be gathered, without permission, based on consumer use of the Internet to develop user profiles to provide targeted online advertising, also known as "behavioral advertising," has raised privacy issues. For an examination of this issue see testimony from hearings "Communications Networks and Consumer Privacy: Recent Developments," held April 23, 2009, by the House Energy and Commerce Subcommittee on Communications, Technology, and the Internet. Available at http://energycommerce.house.gov/.

[47] Network Management Policy. *Announcement Regarding An Amendment to Our Acceptable Use Policy.* Available at http://xfinity.comcast.net/terms/network/amendment/.

[48] If the subscriber does not modify their use and/or the subscriber exceeds the cap again within six months service will be subject to termination and eligibility for either residential or commercial Internet service will be suspended for 12 months. According to Comcast the median data usage by their Internet residential customers is approximately 4-6 GB per month and less than 1% of Comcast customers use an "excessive" amount of data. A customer would have to do any one of the following, Comcast states, to reach the monthly 250 GB limit: send 50 million e-mails (at 0.05 KB/e-mail); download 62,500 songs (at 4 MB/song); download 125 standard-definition movies (at 2 GB/movie); or upload 25,000 hi-resolution digital photos (at 10 MB/photo). For additional information on Comcast's excessive use policy see (continued...)

Comcast announced that it is replacing its 250 GB/per month usage threshold with new flexible usage trials in selected test markets and suspending enforcement of the 250 GB/per month cap in all remaining markets.[49] AT&T adopted usage caps, effective May 2, 2011, for its DSL and U-Verse residential subscribers. DSL subscribers will be subject to a 150 GB/per month usage cap and U-Verse subscribers will be subject to a 250GB/per month data usage cap. Subscribers who exceed the cap three times across the life of the account, not per month, must pay $10 per every 50GB above the subscribed cap.[50] Similarly CenturyLink announced effective February 2012, the decision to place download limits (or caps) on its residential high-speed Internet plans. Usage caps will vary based on the subscriber's plan with a monthly maximum of 150 GB for the 1.5Mbps plan and a monthly cap of 250 GB for plans greater than 1.5Mbps. CenturyLink will contact those who exceed their usage caps, allow you time to reduce your usage, or allow you to upgrade to a higher data service. There are no overage fees or charges for exceeded usage but CenturyLink reserves the right to disconnect service after the third month of excessive usage in a rolling 12-month period.[51]

Some Internet service providers have also initiated usage trials. For example, in 2008, Time Warner Cable established a usage trial in Beaumont, TX, that offered a range of service tiers. The move by Time Warner Cable to expand these trials to four additional locations[52] caused considerable controversy and was deferred.[53] Since then, however, Time Warner has initiated a voluntary usage-based trial in its southern Texas markets. This trial, which was announced in February 2012, addresses customers who are "light users" by offering an optional usage-based plan, called "Essentials." Subscribers can use up to 5GB per month for a $5 discount from the customer's current bill; if they exceed the cap they will be charged $1 for every additional gigabyte, with an overage fee cap of $25 per month. A usage meter, capable of tracking consumption hour by hour, is provided. This is a voluntary trial and an unlimited option, at a flat monthly rate, will continue to be offered and customers will be permitted to switch back and forth between options.[54] Smaller, more regional providers have stated that usage-based pricing models are growing in popularity and will be necessary in the future as the demand for high bandwidth applications increases.[55] For example, one provider, Knology of Kansas, uses such a pricing

---

(...continued)

"Frequently asked Questions about Excessive Use," available at http://customer.comcast.com.

[49] http://customer.comcast.com/help-and-support/internet/common-questions-excessive-use/.

[50] For additional information on AT&T usage policy for residential broadband services see *What Are AT&T's Tiered Pricing Plans, and What Do They Mean to Me?* Available at http://www.att.com/esupport/internet/usage.JSP#fbid= AOrWfWmMh8z.

[51] *CenturyLink Excessive Use Policy FAQ,* available at http://qwest.centurylink.com/internethelp/pdf/EUP.pdf.

[52] Time Warner Cable announced, on April 9, 2009, plans to implement usage-based billing trials in Rochester, New York and Greensboro, North Carolina, in August 2009, and Austin and San Antonio, Texas, in October, 2009. See *Statement from Landel Hobbs, Chief Operating Officer, Time Warner Cable Re: Consumption Based Billing Trials,* April 9, 2009. Available at http://www.timewarnercable.com/corporate/announcements/cbb.html.

[53] Citing "misunderstanding about our trials," Time Warner Cable announced plans to defer implementation of usage-based billing trials in Rochester, New York, Greensboro, North Carolina, and Austin and San Antonio, Texas, to enable "consultation with our customers and other interested parties." See *Time Warner Cable Charts a New Course on Consumption Based Billing Measurement Tools to be Made Available,* April 16, 2009. Available at http://www.timewarnercable.com/Corporate/announcements/cbb.html.

[54] *Launching An Optional Usage-Based Broadband Pricing Plan In Southern Texas,* available at http://www.twcableuntangled.com/2012/02/launching-an-optional-usage-based-pricing-plan-in-southern-texas-2/ 27/2012.

[55] For example see *ACA: Metered Bandwidth Pricing Is Coming,* available at http://www.broadcastingcable.com/ article/print/210247-ACA_Metered_Bandwidth_Pricing_Is_Coming.php.

---

model. Knology of Kansas offers three service levels at 3, 50, or 250 GB per month, with a $1 per Gigabyte overcharge which is levied only after a second over usage.[56]

Reaction to the imposition of data usage caps has been mixed. Supporters of such billing models state that a small percentage of users consume a disproportionately high percentage of bandwidth and that some form of usage-based pricing may benefit the majority of subscribers, particularly those who are light users.[57] Furthermore, they state that offering a range of service tiers at varying prices offers consumers more choice and control over their usage and subsequent costs. The major growth in bandwidth usage, they also claim, places financial pressure on existing networks for both maintenance and expansion, and establishing a pricing system which charges high bandwidth users is more equitable.

Opponents to such billing plans claim that such practices will stifle innovation in high bandwidth applications and are likely to discourage the experimentation with and adoption of new applications and services. Some concerns have also been expressed that a move to metered/usage-based pricing will help to protect the market share for video services, offered in packaged bundles by network broadband service providers, that compete with new applications and if such caps must exist, should be applied to all online video sources. The move to usage-based pricing, they state, will unfairly disadvantage competing online video services and stifle a nascent market since video applications are more bandwidth-intensive. Opponents have also questioned the accuracy of meters, and specific usage limits and overage fees established in specific trials, stating that the former seem to be "arbitrarily low" and the latter "arbitrarily high."[58] Furthermore they state that since network congestion only occurs in specific locations and is temporary, monthly data caps are not a good measure of congestion causation. Citing the generally falling costs of network equipment and the stability of profit margins, they also question the claims of network broadband operators that increased revenues streams are needed to supply the necessary capital to invest in new infrastructure to meet the growing demand for high bandwidth applications.[59]

The Policy Debate

Questions over the FCC's authority to regulate broadband services under its Title I ancillary authority, and what is perceived by some as inadequacies in the Open Internet Order, have caused some policymakers to support more specific regulatory guidelines to protect the marketplace from potential abuses; a consensus on what these should specifically entail, however, has yet to form. Others feel that that the FCC has overstepped its authority and that the regulation of the Internet is not only unnecessary but harmful. They claim that existing laws regarding competitive behavior are sufficient to deal with potential anti-competitive behavior.

---

[56] Additional bandwidth can be purchased in advance at 10 GB for $10 per month or 50 GB for $25 per month. For additional information on Knology of Kansas bandwidth management see http://www.Kansas.Knology.Com/bandwidth/.

[57] For example, Time Warner states that the top 25% of its users consume 100 times more bandwidth than the bottom 25% and 30% of its high speed Internet service (i.e., Road Runner) customers use less than 1 GB (Gigabyte) per month. See *Consumption Based Billing FAQs*. Available at http://www.timewarnercable.com/corporate/announcements/cbb_faq.html.

[58] See Free Press letter to House Energy and Commerce Committee, April 22, 2009. Available at http://www.Freepress.net/files/FP_metering_letter.pdf.

[59] *As Costs Fall, Companies Push to Raise Internet Price*, New York Times, April 20, 2009. Available at http://www.nytimes.com/2009/04/20/business/20isp.html?_r=1.

The issue of net neutrality, and whether legislation is needed to ensure access to broadband networks and services, has become a major focal point in the debate over telecommunications reform.[60] Those opposed to the enactment of legislation to impose specific Internet network access or "net neutrality" mandates claim that such action goes against the long-standing policy to keep the Internet as free as possible from regulation. They have claimed that the imposition of such requirements is not only unnecessary, but would have negative consequences for the deployment and advancement of broadband facilities. For example, further expansion of networks by existing providers and the entrance of new network providers would be discouraged, they claim, as investors would be less willing to finance networks that may be operating under mandatory build-out and/or access requirements. Application innovation could also be discouraged, they contend, if, for example, network providers are restricted in the way they manage their networks or are limited in their ability to offer new service packages or formats. Such legislation is not needed, they claim, as major Internet access providers have stated publicly that they are committed to upholding the FCC's four policy principles.[61] Opponents also state that advocates of regulation cannot point to any widespread behavior that justifies the need to establish such regulations and note that competition between telephone and cable system providers, as well as the growing presence of new technologies (e.g., satellite, wireless, and power lines), will serve to counteract any potential anti-competitive behavior. Furthermore, opponent's claim, even if such a violation should occur, the FCC already has the needed authority to pursue violators. They note, for example, that the FCC has successfully used its existing authority in a March 3, 2005, action against Madison River Communications. In this case, the FCC intervened and resolved, through a consent decree, an alleged case of port blocking by Madison River Communications, a local exchange (telephone) company.[62] The full force of antitrust law is also available, they claim, in cases of discriminatory behavior.

Proponents of net neutrality legislation, however, feel that absent some regulation, Internet access providers will become gatekeepers and use their market power to the disadvantage of Internet users and competing content and application providers. They also cite concerns that the Internet could develop into a two-tiered system favoring large, established businesses or those with ties to broadband network providers. While market forces should be a deterrent to such anti-competitive behavior, they point out that the market for residential broadband delivery has traditionally been dominated by two providers, the telephone and cable television companies.[63] The need to formulate a national policy to clarify expectations and ensure the "openness" of the Internet is important to protect the benefits and promote the further expansion of broadband, they claim. The adoption of a single, coherent, regulatory framework to prevent discrimination, supporters claim,

---

[60] For a more lengthy discussion regarding proponents' and opponents' views see, for example, testimony from Senate Commerce Committee hearings on Net Neutrality, February 7, 2006. Available at http://commerce.senate.gov/public/ index.cfm?FuseAction=Hearings.Hearing&Hearing_ID=1708.

[61] See testimony of Kyle McSlarrow, President and CEO of the National Cable and Telecommunications Association, and Walter McCormick, President and CEO of the United States Telecom Association, hearing on Net Neutrality before the Senate Commerce Committee, February 7, 2006, cited above.

[62] The FCC entered into a consent decree with Madison River Communications to settle charges that the company had deliberately blocked the ports on its network that were used by Vonage Corp. to provide voice over Internet protocol (VoIP) service. Under terms of the decree Madison River agreed to pay a $15,000 fine and not block ports used for VoIP applications. See http://hraunfoss.fcc.gov/edocs_public/attachmatch/DA-05-543A2.pdf. for a copy of the consent decree.

[63] Some point to the growth in mobile wireless subscribers with data plans for full Internet access as a growing third provider. For FCC market share data for high-speed connections see *Internet Access Services: Status as of June 30, 2011*, Federal Communications Commission, Industry Analysis and Technology Division, Wireline Competition Bureau, released June 2012. See http://hraunfoss.fcc.gov/edocs_public/attachmatch/DOC-314630A1.pdf.

---

would be a positive step for further development of the Internet, by providing the marketplace stability needed to encourage investment and innovation which will foster the growth of new services and applications. Furthermore, they state that there have been cases where ISPs have abused their market power[64] and relying on current laws and case-by-case anti-trust-like enforcement, they claim, is too cumbersome, slow, and expensive, particularly for small start-up enterprises.[65]

Congressional Activity

112th Congress

A consensus on the net neutrality issue has remained elusive and support for the FCC's Open Internet Order has been mixed. (See "The FCC Open Internet Order," above.) While some Members of Congress support the action and in some cases would have supported an even stronger approach, others feel that the FCC has overstepped its authority and that the regulation of the Internet is not only unnecessary, but harmful. Internet regulation and the FCC's authority to implement such regulations has been a topic of legislation (H.R. 96, H.R. 166, S. 74, H.R. 2434, H.R. 1, H.R. 3630, H.J.Res. 37, S.J.Res. 6) and hearings (Senate Commerce Committee, House Communications Subcommittee, and House Intellectual Property, Competition, and the Internet Subcommittee) in the 112th Congress.

Legislation to limit FCC regulation has been introduced. H.R. 96, the "Internet Freedom Act," introduced, on January 5, 2011, by Representative Blackburn and 59 additional original cosponsors, prohibits, with exceptions, the FCC from proposing, promulgating, or issuing any regulations regarding the Internet or IP-enabled services, effective the date of the bill's enactment. Exceptions are made for regulations that the FCC determines are necessary to prevent damage to national security, to ensure the public safety, or to assist or facilitate actions taken by a federal or state law enforcement agency. The bill also contains a finding that the Internet and IP-enabled services are services affecting interstate commerce and are not subject to State or municipality jurisdiction. Another measure, H.R. 166, the "Internet Investment, Innovation, and Competition Preservation Act," introduced on January 5, 2011, by Representative Stearns, requires the FCC to prove the existence of a "market failure" before regulating information services or Internet access services. The FCC must also conclude that the "market failure" is causing "specific, identified harm to consumers" and that regulations are necessary to ameliorate that harm. The bill also contains provisions that require any FCC regulation to be the "least restrictive," determine that the benefits exceed the cost, permit network management, not prohibit managed services, be reviewed every two years, and be subject to sunset. Any such regulation is required to be enforced on a nondiscriminatory basis between and among broadband network, service, application, and content providers. A more narrowly focused limitation was contained within H.R. 3630, the "Middle Class Tax Relief and Job Creation Act of 2011" as passed (234-193) by the House on December 13, 2011. Section 4105 of Title IV (spectrum provisions) of the bill prohibits the FCC from imposing network access/management requirements on licensees. More specifically, the

---

[64] For example, see the mentioned Comcast and the Madison River cases, discussed above.

[65] For example, see testimony of Vint Cerf, VP Google, Earl Comstock, President and CEO of CompTel, and Jeffrey Citron, Chairman and CEO Vonage, hearing on Net Neutrality, before the Senate Commerce Committee, February 7, 2006, cited above.

provision prohibited the promulgation of auction service rules that restrict a licensee's ability to manage network traffic or prioritize the traffic on its network, or that would require providing network access on a wholesale basis. However, the provision was removed from the bill prior to final passage (P.L. 112-96).

Legislation to strengthen the FCC's ability to regulate open access by amending Title II of the 1934 Communications Act has also been introduced. S. 74, the "Internet Freedom, Broadband Promotion, and Consumer Protection Act of 2011," introduced, January 25, 2011, by Senator Cantwell, provides for strengthened open access protections. More specifically the bill contains among its provisions those that codify the four FCC principles issued in 2005 as well as those to require Internet service providers to be nondiscriminatory regarding access and transparent in their network management practices. The bill also requires Internet service providers to provide service to end users upon "reasonable request" and offer stand-alone broadband access at "reasonable rates, terms, and conditions" and prohibits Internet service providers from requiring paid prioritization. The bill's requirements apply to both wireline and wireless platforms; however, the FCC is allowed to take into consideration difference in network technologies when applying requirements. The FCC is tasked with establishing the necessary rules and injured parties can be awarded damages by the FCC or a federal district court.

Other measures, which proved unsuccessful, were considered to prevent, or at least delay, implementation of the FCC's Open Internet Order. Attempts were made, through the appropriations process, to add language that would prevent the FCC from using its funds to implement the Open Internet Order. Language attached to the FY2011 appropriation measure, H.R. 1, to prevent the use of FCC FY2011 funds for implementation of the order was passed by the House. The Continuing Appropriations Act, 2011 (H.R. 1) passed (235-189) by the House on February 19, 2011, contained an amendment, introduced by Representative Walden and passed by the House (244-181), to prohibit the FCC from using any funds made available by the act to implement the FCC's Open Internet Order adopted on December 21, 2010. No such provision, however, was included in the final FY2011 appropriations bill, H.R. 1473, passed by Congress and signed by the President (P.L. 112-10). Similarly language included in the FY2012 Financial Services and General Government Appropriations bill (H.R. 2434), which includes funding for the FCC, contained a provision that barred the FCC from using any funds to implement its Open Internet Order adopted December 21, 2010. This measure passed the House Appropriations Committee on June 23, 2011 (H.Rept. 112-136)[66] but no such provision was included in the final FY2012 consolidated appropriations bill, H.R. 2055, which was signed by President Obama (P.L. 112-74) on December 23, 2011.

Another approach, using the Congressional Review Act to overturn the order,[67] was also under consideration. Identical resolutions of disapproval were introduced, on February 16, 2011, in both the House (H.J.Res. 37) and Senate (S.J.Res. 6). These measures state that Congress disapproves of the rule submitted by the FCC's report and order relating to the matter of preserving the open Internet and broadband industry practices adopted by the FCC on December 21, 2010, and further

---

[66] The Senate Appropriations subcommittee-passed (September 14, 2011) appropriations measure, S. 1573, did contain a provision to prohibit the FCC from using funds to implement the Open Internet Order, but it did not remain in the full committee passed (September 15, 2011) version (S.Rept. 112-79).

[67] Under the Congressional Review Act (CRA; 5 U.S.C. paras.801-808) Congress is given 60 in-session-days, from publication in the *Federal Register* or submission to Congress, whichever is later, to review and potentially overturn federal agency major rulemakings. For a further discussion of the CRA see CRS Report R40997, *Congressional Review Act: Rules Not Submitted to GAO and Congress*, by Curtis W. Copeland.

states that "such rule would have no force or effect." A hearing on H.J.Res. 37 was held by the House Energy and Commerce Communications and Technology Subcommittee on March 9, 2011, and the Subcommittee passed the measure (15-8), on a party-line vote, immediately following the hearing. On March 25, 2011, the House Energy and Commerce Committee passed (30-23) H.J.Res. 37. On April 8, 2011, the full House considered and passed (240-179) H.J.Res. 37. However an identical resolution of disapproval (S.J.Res. 6) failed to pass the Senate on November 10, 2011, by a 52-46 vote.

111th Congress

Although the 111th Congress saw considerable activity addressing the net neutrality debate, no final action was taken. One stand-alone measure (H.R. 3458) that comprehensively addressed the net neutrality debate was introduced in the 111th Congress. H.R. 3458, the "Internet Freedom Preservation Act of 2009," introduced by Representative Edward Markey, and also supported by then-House Energy and Commerce Committee Chairman Waxman, sought to establish a national policy of nondiscrimination and openness with respect to Internet access offered to the public. The bill also required the offering of unbundled, or stand-alone, Internet access service as well as transparency for the consuming public with respect to speed, nature, and limitations on service offerings and the public disclosure of network management practices. The FCC was tasked with promulgating the rules relating to the enforcement and implementation of the legislation. Then-House Communications, Technology, and the Internet Subcommittee Chairman Boucher stated that he continued to work with broadband providers and content providers to seek common ground on network management practices, and chose to pursue that approach.[68] Furthermore, the Senate Commerce and House Energy and Commerce Committees and Communications Subcommittees held a series of staff-led sessions with industry stakeholders to discuss a range of communications policies including broadband regulation and FCC authority.[69]

Two bills (S. 1836, H.R. 3924) were introduced in response to the adoption, by the FCC, of a NPR on preserving the open Internet. S. 1836, introduced on October 22, 2009, by Senator McCain, prohibited, with some exceptions, the FCC from proposing, promulgating, or issuing any further regulations regarding the Internet or IP-enabled services. Exceptions included those relating to national security, public safety, federal or state law enforcement, and Universal Service Fund solvency.[70] Additional provisions reaffirmed that existing regulations, including those relating to CALEA, remain in force and stated as a general principle, that the Internet and all IP-enable services are services affecting interstate commerce and are not subject to State or municipal locality jurisdiction. H.R. 3924, introduced by Representative Blackburn on October 26, 2009, was identical to S. 1836, except for title and the omission of the reference to the Universal Service Fund. H.Con.Res. 311, introduced by Representative Gene Green and 49 other House Members on July 30, 2010, affirmed that it is the responsibility of Congress to determine the regulatory authority of the FCC with respect to broadband Internet services and called upon

---

[68] *Boucher Opts For Talks, Not Legislation, On Net Neutrality,* National Journal, Congress Daily, February 26, 2009. *Boucher, Stakeholders Working On Network Management Issues,* Telecommunications Reports, March 15, 2009, p. 19.

[69] *Bicameral Bipartisan Telecommunications Update Statement.* U.S. Senate Committee on Commerce, Science and Transportation. Press Release June 18, 2010. Available at http://democrats.energycommerce.house.gov/index.php?q= news/bicameral-bipartisan-telecommunications-update-statement, June 2010.

[70] For a discussion and analysis of issues regarding the Universal Service Fund see CRS Report RL33979, *Universal Service Fund: Background and Options for Reform,* by Angele A. Gilroy.

the FCC to suspend any further action on its proceedings until such time as Congress delegates such authority to the FCC.

Another measure (H.R. 5257) introduced by Representative Stearns, addressed the possible reclassification of broadband service and would required, among other provisions, that the FCC prove the existence of a "market failure" before regulating information services or Internet access services. Furthermore the bill required, among other provisions, that the FCC conclude that the market failure is causing "specific, identified harm to consumers" and if devising regulations must adopt those that are the "least restrictive," permit network management, and are subject to sunset. Still another measure (S. 3624), introduced by Senator DeMint, contained provisions that required the FCC to prove consumers are being substantially harmed by a lack of marketplace choice before imposing new regulations and must weigh the potential cost of action against any benefits to consumers or competition. The FCC was given the authority to hear complaints for violations and award damages to injured parties. The bill also required that any rules the FCC adopted would sunset in five years unless it could make the same finding again.

The net neutrality issue was also narrowly addressed within the context of the American Recovery and Reinvestment Act of 2009 (ARRA, P.L. 111-5). The ARRA contains provisions that require the National Telecommunications and Information Administration (NTIA), in consultation with the FCC, to establish "nondiscrimination and network interconnection obligations" as a requirement for grant participants in the Broadband Technology Opportunities Program (BTOP). The law further directs that the FCC's four broadband policy principles, issued in August 2005, are the minimum obligations to be imposed.[71] These obligations were issued July 1, 2009, in conjunction with the release of the notice of funds availability (NOFA) soliciting applications for the program. (See "The American Recovery and Reinvestment Act of 2009," above, for details.) The FCC's *National Broadband Plan* (NBP), which was required to be written in compliance with provisions contained in the ARRA, while making no recommendations, did contain discussions regarding the open Internet and the classification of information services. (See "The FCC's National Broadband Plan," above.)

Concern over the move by some broadband network providers to expand their implementation of metered or consumption-based billing prompted the introduction of legislation (H.R. 2902) to provide for oversight of volume usage service plans. H.R. 2902, the "Broadband Internet Fairness Act," introduced by former Representative Massa, required, among its provisions, that any broadband Internet service provider, serving 2 million or more subscribers, submit any volume usage based service plan, which the provider is proposing or offering, to the Federal Trade Commission (FTC) for approval. The FTC, in consultation with the FCC, was required to review such plans "to ensure that such plans are fairly based on cost." Such plans were subject to agency review and public hearings. Plans determined by the FTC to impose "rates, terms, and conditions that are unjust, unreasonable, or unreasonably discriminatory" were to be declared unlawful. Violators were subject to injunctive relief requiring the suspension, termination, or revision of such plans and were subject to a fine of not more than $1 million.

---

[71] For a further more detailed discussion of the broadband infrastructure programs contained in P.L. 111-5 see CRS Report R40436, *Broadband Infrastructure Programs in the American Recovery and Reinvestment Act*, by Lennard G. Kruger.

Author Contact Information

Angele A. Gilroy
Specialist in Telecommunications Policy
agilroy@crs.loc.gov, 7-7778